Praise for Th

"With her trademark wit and
breaks down the complicated elements involved in being a trustee. She explains the rewards and responsibilities of this position in plain English, making this a must-read for anyone acting as trustee or considering becoming one."

—**Susan R. Lipp,** Editor-in-Chief, *Trusts & Estates*

"A great starting point—or refresher—for understanding trusts. Patricia Angus has distilled the essential elements of how a trust works and the roles of trustees and beneficiaries by drawing on her extensive experience as an attorney and advisor to those who create, manage, and benefit from trusts. I recommend this primer to anyone embarking on being a trustee."

—**Don Kozusko,** Partner, Kozusko Harris Duncan, and Fellow, American College of Trust and Estate Counsel

"At last! A warm and honest voice encouraging the reader in clear-speak (not jargon) exactly how to navigate the daunting world of trusts and money. The length, the clear examples, and Patricia's instructions—from a warm and friendly coach who's luckily also an expert—create a most powerful primer that is accessible to all."

—**Charlotte Beyer,** Founder, Institute for Private Investors, and author, *Wealth Management Unwrapped*

"A few people, who embody the virtues of fidelity, caring, and humility, will be asked to be trustees. Patricia Angus has written *The Trustee Primer: A Guide for Personal Trustees* to offer these people of special character a way of understanding what it means to be a trustee and what acting as trustee entails.

She has made a complex legal relationship into a comprehensible set of human and legal relationships that will help every person who might act as a trustee, or who is already serving, become a great trustee. It will also help such great trustees in turn help bring great beneficiaries to life."

—**James (Jay) E. Hughes, Jr.**, author, *Family Wealth: Keeping it in the Family*, *Family: The Compact Among Generations*, and co-author, *Family Trusts*

"Although Patricia Angus wrote *The Trustee Primer* primarily for potential and current trustees, it is practical and understandable for people in several stakeholder groups. Parents and grandparents often create trusts primarily to preserve the family's financial capital without having a deep understanding of the long-term impact of those trusts on their families. Family members and friends are often asked to serve as trustees without really knowing what that entails. Generations of family members are beneficiaries of trusts without much understanding of how their trusts work. Patricia's primer lays out a logical, step-by-step process for how to think about the opportunities and challenges associated with serving as a trustee. She explains terminology clearly and puts complex trust law into the context of serving as a trustee. The worksheet incorporated throughout the text is a useful tool to translate the content into the reader's immediate circumstance and decision-making process. I highly recommend this primer for clients and colleagues."

—**Bonnie Brown Hartley,** President, Transition Dynamics Inc, co-author of *Family Wealth Transition Planning* and co-author of the international thriller *Broken Trust*

The TRUSTEE PRIMER

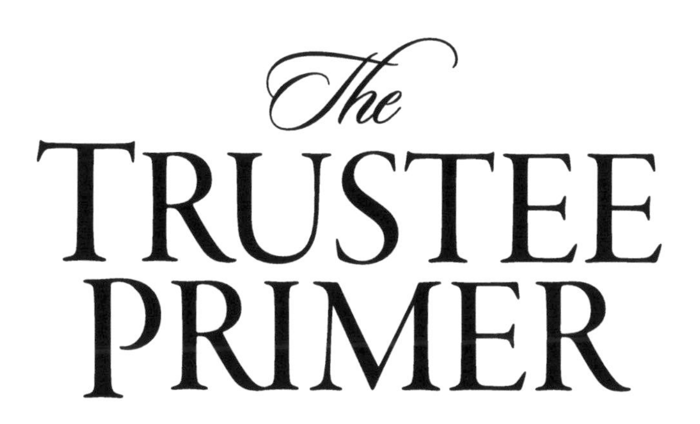

A Guide for Personal Trustees

PATRICIA M. ANGUS, ESQ.

The Trustee Primer: *A Guide for Personal Trustees*

ISBN: 978-0-9970680-0-9

Edited by Susan B. Weiner, CFA
Copy editing by thinkStory.biz
Book design by AuthorSupport.com

For information please contact Angus Advisory Group LLC via email at: contact@angusadvisorygroup.com.

Contents

Contents (CONTINUED)

Introduction

Have you been asked to serve as a trustee? Are you acting as one for a friend or family member? If so, you might have felt a surge of pride and satisfaction when you were first asked. Perhaps you thought, "My friend trusts me more than I realized." You might have also experienced a sense of duty or obligation ("If my father thinks I can do this, then I can. I wouldn't dare not do it."). If you are like most people, you have been chosen because of your close relationship with the person who appointed you or you are seen as someone who is especially trustworthy and competent. Congratulations! This should make you feel very good.

After this rush of positive feelings, you might have some more complicated, and often conflicting, sensations. Of course, you know you are competent and trustworthy. Yes, it is right that you were chosen. But maybe you're not sure whether you actually want to be a trustee, or even whether you are well suited, or have the time, to do it. Deep down you might hear a voice that sounds like the robot in the American TV classic *Lost in Space*, which blasted out, "Danger, Will Robinson!" and flailed its arms when it sensed that something untoward was about to happen. You don't have to look too far in the media or even in your circle of family and friends to hear about a trust situation that ended with damaged relationships or a court battle. That's pretty scary.

This primer has been written for you. It provides information about being a trustee to help you understand what you might be getting into and how you can do it well. It will even give you a chance to consider whether trusteeship suits you and what to do if it's not a good fit.

But before going further, let me tell you three things.

First, your initial instincts are absolutely correct. It is a great honor to be asked to serve as a trustee. In fact, there are very few things you can do—under the law at least—that have a higher level of responsibility toward another person. You have been given an opportunity to have a profound impact on the life of someone who is already or could become very dear to you and to do this on behalf of someone in your inner circle. Being a trustee puts you in an intimate relationship that is like being family, but in many ways can be better. You are in a position to potentially guide, and mentor, and learn from someone who may or may not be related to you. Everything you do as trustee will affect this person's life, and if done with humility and compassion, it will likely be for the better. You have a chance to listen to the person's hopes and challenges and provide encouragement as that person journeys through life. Rather than merely smoothing the road ahead, you can ride along together for a little while, point out potential bumps and detours, and enjoy some beautiful views. You will learn new things and undoubtedly will teach a bit, too. As one trustee put it, "I became a part of my nephew's life in a way that I never would have otherwise. I wouldn't trade it for the world."

Second, your gut is also telling you something important. Being a trustee is not to be taken lightly. There are laws upon laws that govern what you must do, and if you do not follow them well, serious consequences can result. *Liability* is a word that you will need to learn more about, as your personal and financial wellbeing will be on the line the entire time you are trustee, and even afterwards. This primer will touch briefly on these issues, and you will need to gather more resources as time goes along. Protecting yourself is essential to your new role. Further, the risks go far beyond legal liability. You can inadvertently harm the very person whom you are trying to help. Trust your gut—it is telling you about this very real possibility.

Third, your best chance to make an informed decision about whether to accept the appointment and to do a good job as a trustee is to gain the right knowledge from the outset. While this might be the first time that you are serving as a trustee, you are not the first person to act in this role. People have been doing it for centuries. That said, you should know that you have a way out. If you don't want to take on the position, that's okay. But before you head for the exit, I encourage you to begin here, with the reassurance that more detailed resources are available when you are ready for them and there are professionals who can help you.

This primer is divided into four sections focusing on questions likely to be on your mind. You can read it straight through or start with the questions that most concern you. Part I covers the trust concept and basic vocabulary. Part II goes into your primary responsibilities and duties. Part III highlights the beneficiary's role and position, and Part IV wraps up with some final questions to consider before you agree to accept, or continue, your role as trustee.

PART I

Trust Concept and Basic Vocabulary

WHAT IS A TRUST?

You may be one of the fortunate few who have been named as trustee after having had some experience with trusts. For many people, however, it is like jumping into the deep end of the pool without a single swimming class. In this case, you don't even know what a pool is or what's in it. To start, you must get a handle on the concept of a trust itself. It is deceptively simple, but differs from many of the basic ideas of property, ownership, and relationships that you may be familiar with so far.

In the most basic sense, a trust is a set of legal relationships among several parties. It's not simply a contract, although it might seem like one. It's not an investment account, but may have investment accounts in it. It's not a hierarchical power structure, although many have used it for their own power trips. Rather, it is a wonderful creation of the law that provides a way to take care of people and property within a time-tested framework and guidelines. This unique arrangement has centuries' worth of laws defining each party's roles and responsibilities. You, as trustee, are one of the most important persons involved. This is what it looks like:

Visualizing Your Trust

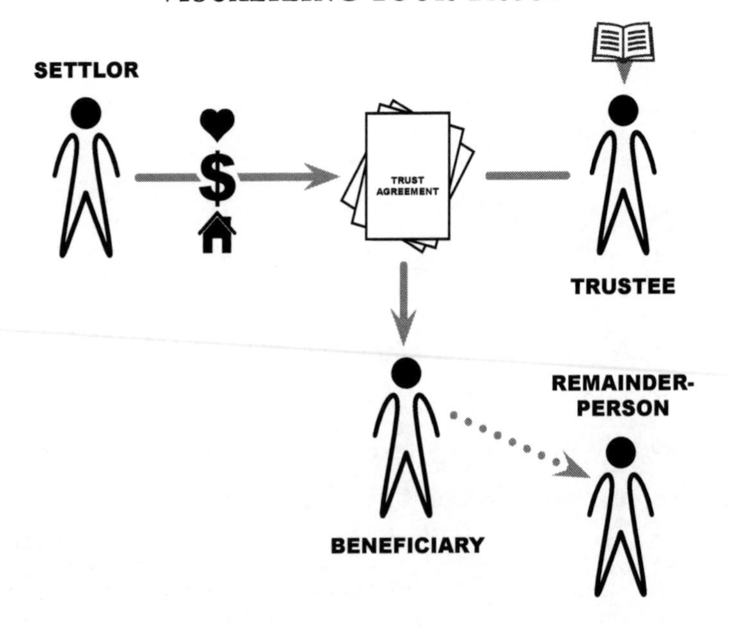

- The **settlor** (aka creator, trustor, donor, or grantor) establishes and funds the trust and puts instructions for what to do with the trust fund in a **trust agreement**.
- The **trustee** administers, invests, and distributes the trust fund according to the trust agreement.
- The **beneficiary** receives the benefits through distributions from the trust.
- When the trust ends, a **remainderperson** receives whatever is left in it.

It helps to use the proper words for each role to keep the relationships in perspective and to remind all parties of the differences in their respective positions. A trust can have multiple trustees, beneficiaries, and remainderpersons; yours may have one or more of each. Also, it is quite possible that you may serve with one or more co-trustees (companies or individuals). In that case, and more generally, you will need to adapt these basic building blocks of information to your situation.

WHY DO TRUSTS EXIST?

A little history might help you understand how this works. It is said that the law of trusts developed in the United Kingdom nine hundred or so years ago, during the Middle Ages. At that time, it was common for a landowner (who could only be male) to leave his property (and wife and family) for months at a time when he went off to war, i.e., the Crusades. In the beginning, many of these Crusaders would leave their property in the hands of a (male) neighbor or friend while away, so that someone could take care of the land, defend it against others, and pay any taxes due. This seemed to be a good idea until a Crusader returned and encountered resistance to getting the property back. Or, in other cases, if he had not made prior arrangements, he might find that a stranger had taken over while he was gone. Either way, it was not a happy homecoming, and the family was certainly not safe in the interim. So, the returning Crusaders would seek help from the courts to get ownership back.

In the beginning, the law couldn't really handle this situation. It didn't have a simple answer for who the owner was. It might recognize the friend, neighbor, or stranger as the current owner, leaving the original owner out in the cold. This did not seem fair. While it took some time to get there, the courts and consequently the law created a better solution to this complicated problem. The way they did it changed the law of property forever and established the basic format of trusts that exist today.

Put simply, the solution was to split the concept of ownership into two: a *legal* owner and a *beneficial* owner. One person would be recognized as the legal owner with the right—and responsibility—to pay the bills and maintain the property; another person became the beneficial owner, that is, the only person who could actually benefit from the property. The Crusader's friend or neighbor became the legal owner, with the right and responsibility of maintaining the property. His wife and children became beneficial owners who could maintain access, use, and the benefits of the property. Anyone who is involved in trusts must understand this distinction. Neither party has full and complete rights over the trust. Both share ownership, from a legal standpoint at least, in a way that is meant to be practical and enforceable. This concept is now recognized as an ingenious solution to commonly occurring problems and has gradually been adopted in various forms by most of the developed and developing economies in the world.

Let's take a straightforward example to bring it into modern times. Imagine that Susan, an adult, wants to use some of her resources to take care of her nephew, Bob, who is ten years old. It might seem easiest if she could just give him the money directly or transfer it into a bank account in his name. But she knows that won't work. Bob is still a child and can't have a bank account, and the money would be at risk in his hands. Her solution is to ask her friend Trent if he could hold the funds for Bob and use them only for Bob's sake. She writes out specific instructions for when and how Trent should give them to Bob or use them for his benefit, for example, to pay for school or medical expenses. Further, she documents the instructions in a trust agreement. She realizes that the funds might outlast Bob's lifetime, so she includes a contingency plan: anything left when Bob dies is to be given to Roger, another child she would like to support in the future. In this case, Susan is the settlor, Trent is the trustee, and Bob the beneficiary. Roger is the remainderperson.

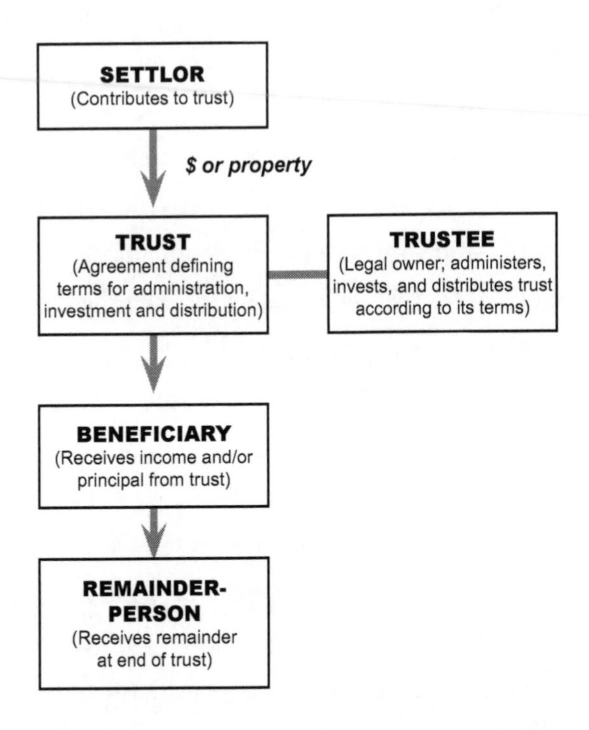

Now that you know the basic concept, the next step is to figure out how this set of relationships applies to you.

Who are the key parties in your trust?

It's never too soon to identify the key parties in your trust. In your case, the settlor is the person who has asked you to help out as trustee with some assets called the *trust fund.*

If you have been asked to be a trustee, you probably know the identity of the settlor of your trust. If you don't, you will need to find out. This is a good time to look at the "Your Trust" sheet at the back of this primer. It provides space to record the important information that you should always have on hand. You might want to begin completing it now.

You will be responsible for following the instructions the settlor has provided in a trust agreement on how you are to take care of the beneficiary.

It would be good if you could record the name of the beneficiary as well. The trust agreement will identify this person by name or possibly by category such as "the settlor's child(ren)."

When the trust ends, you will have to deliver any remaining property to a remainderperson. Generally speaking, trustees must balance the interests of a current beneficiary with those of future remainderpersons.

The trust agreement will identify the remainderperson, either by name or possibly by category of people such as "the settlor's grandchild(ren)." You should record it now.

Trusts often last longer than the period in which a trustee serves in that capacity. For this reason, trust agreements often set out the process for the appointment of a successor trustee in case a trustee declines, resigns, or can no longer serve due to incapacity or death. If the trust agreement does not include this provision, and even if it does, the governing law also provides guidance.

You should know whether and how your successor will be appointed as trustee. Review the trust agreement and record that information in the "Your Trust" sheet.

Now that you know who the key parties are in your trust, let's step back for a minute and focus on why you are all in this together, so that you can put these concepts into perspective.

What is the purpose of your trust?

Before you think about what you have to do as trustee, you must consider why you are doing it in the first place. Without the "why," the "what" can seem meaningless. It is anything but that. While it might seem obvious that there would be a stated purpose behind the creation of every trust, it might not be easy to figure it out. In fact, many trust agreements do not mention their purpose.

Further, each trust is unique. Even two trusts with the exact same wording can be different. Don't believe any press or sales pitch that describes trusts as "products" you can buy off the shelf. Trust agreements often contain a lot of boilerplate text, but do not be misled by that—trusts are anything but routine. Their purpose—or rather, purposes—are multiple and complex; life-giving and lifetime transcending; general and specific.

Speaking generally, every trust must have a positive purpose; otherwise, why would anyone go to all the effort of creating it? By this I mean "positive" with respect to the people involved. It must make their lives better, in a deeper sense beyond financial or transactional considerations. Put simply, the general purpose of any trust is to make the lives of the grantor, settlor, and beneficiary better than they would have been without it. Not simply better because they have more money—it's clear that's not a guarantee of a happy or fulfilling life. Rather, grantors seek comfort that their goals of providing for beneficiaries have a way of coming to fruition. Trustees can find deep meaning in their role, and beneficiaries can work in tandem with the trustee as they pursue their lives in a meaningful way.

Of course, there are other, more specific, purposes for many trusts. The most obvious are those that are set up to minimize taxes. For example, in the United States many settlors use trusts to pass assets across generations while minimizing estate taxes. But even these trusts will differ from each other, depending on which family members are named as beneficiaries, what assets are contributed to the trusts, and any other intentions the settlor had in mind when the trust was initiated. For example, a trust that owns a family business will have a very different purpose from one that holds stocks, even if both had tax motivations. The trust might be intended to own the family business for a group of family members; the stocks might merely be investment strategies.

More importantly, taxes are not the only reason that trusts are established. One of the most common and compelling reasons to create a trust is to provide for children in case their parents die prematurely. Others are established to provide professional management of assets for surviving spouses or beneficiaries who might not have investment experience. Trusts have been used to create some of the largest and smallest charitable ventures in the world.

As trustee you must find out the purpose, especially the positive one, for your trust as soon as possible. That seems like a simple task, but in many cases figuring it out can be harder than you might imagine. A good place to start is the trust agreement itself, even if it feels like a bit of a scavenger hunt. Look for language in the first paragraphs or pages that states the settlor's intentions and goals. If there is no language (and even if there is), it would be ideal to speak with the settlor and learn about the trust purpose. If you are unable to ask the settlor, you may be able to ask the lawyers or other professionals who were involved when the trust was devised. You may never know exactly what the settlor had in mind, but even a little guidance will go a long way. Always keep in mind that there must be a positive purpose for the trust, even if implicit.

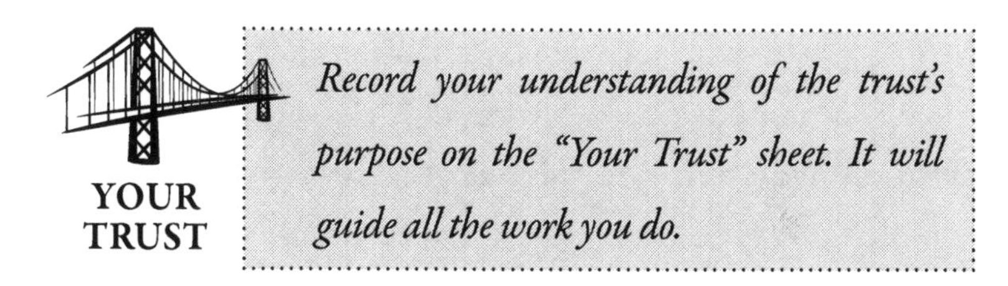

Record your understanding of the trust's purpose on the "Your Trust" sheet. It will guide all the work you do.

Now that you have explored the purpose of your trust, you are ready to learn about another important concept—whether the trust can be changed or cancelled.

Can the trust be revoked?

It is essential that you know whether your trust can be changed or cancelled. This will help you fully understand your powers, as trustee, and how they relate to any powers remaining with the settlor or others. This hinges on whether the trust is *revocable* or *irrevocable*, as follows:

1. Revocable Trust. A trust is revocable if the person who created it retains the right to revoke (from the Latin *revocare*, meaning "cancel" or "call back") the trust and thereby take the trust fund back. In most revocable trusts, this can be done at any time and without anyone's consent; in some, there are stated limits or consents required. Revocable trusts are often used to hold assets that will transfer outside the probate court system, which oversees the transfer of one's property at death. In some states this saves costs and in most cases it saves time for the surviving family members. Revocable trusts are also an effective way to hold wealth so that property management is not disrupted in the event of the settlor's incapacity. In the United States, revocable trusts generally do not provide protection against creditors and do not provide tax benefits. Assets of a revocable trust are considered for tax purposes to be owned directly by the settlor; the settlor must pay taxes on any income, which is reported on the settlor's income tax return. In that case, as trustee you will be responsible for providing the settlor with information on the financial activities in the trust.

2. Irrevocable Trust. The settlor of an irrevocable trust generally cannot revoke or cancel the trust. This kind of trust can be created during life (and if so, might be referred to as *inter vivos*, meaning between living persons) or at death. If established during life, the trust is created using a document signed by the settlor and trustee. Generally, its assets will not be subject to probate, so it is a way to set up a mechanism to transfer assets during life and also receive assets at death that will continue in trust after the settlor's death.

Alternatively, an irrevocable trust can be created at death in two ways. It can be written into a person's last will and testament and, if so, is known as a *testamentary trust*. It can also be written in an *inter vivos trust* created by the settlor during life. Any trust that was revocable during the settlor's life becomes irrevocable at the settlor's death because, logically, the settlor is no longer capable of revoking it. In the United States, as trustee you will be responsible for tax reporting on behalf of the trust and providing information to beneficiaries who will have to report income received from the trust on their tax returns. Further, you may have state reporting requirements that can differ depending on whether the trust is an inter vivos or testamentary trust.

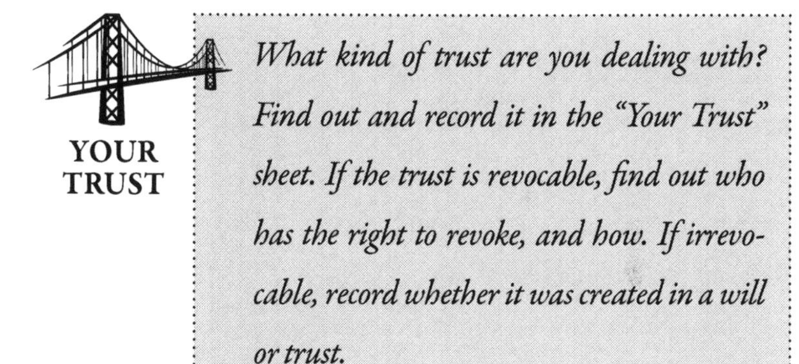

What kind of trust are you dealing with? Find out and record it in the "Your Trust" sheet. If the trust is revocable, find out who has the right to revoke, and how. If irrevocable, record whether it was created in a will or trust.

Now that you know what kind of trust you have, there is one final concept to cover before moving forward.

WHAT IS THE TRUST FUND?

As trustee, you will be in charge of handling the trust fund, consisting of *principal* and *income*, two terms which have specific meanings in the world of trusts. Before you get too far into the details, it would help to understand why the distinction between these two concepts—principal and income—matters so much.

First, anyone who is checking to make sure that a trust has been handled appropriately will want to see records that distinguish between trust income and principal. This includes courts, beneficiaries, and other legal authorities.

Second, many trusts provide that one beneficiary, or group of beneficiaries, is entitled to receive trust income while others can only receive distributions of principal. This is often the case in so-called marital trusts in the United States, where a surviving spouse must receive all income from the trust to comply with tax regulations and principal might be left for children who are living at the spouse's death. In other cases, a trust might be set up to hold a family business, with the beneficiaries only receiving profits generated by the business, as opposed to the value of the business itself, unless or until it is later sold.

Third, taxation of the trust is closely tied to the nature of the assets and whether they are considered income or principal. This part of the U.S. Internal Revenue Code contains some of its most complicated provisions; tax laws in other jurisdictions can be equally opaque.

So, what are trust income and principal? The initial funding of the trust is known as principal, or if you prefer Latin, *corpus*. For example, if a trust is funded with a stock, its value on the date of transfer is the trust principal. It would seem logical that any dividends generated by the stock would be considered income, and that is generally true. But income for trust purposes is not always so easy to identify, as we'll explore more fully in Part II. In fact, for a trust the definition of income is determined by the law governing the trust (most often the state in the United States where the trust is located or the country if elsewhere) and may vary from the usual interest and dividends that you might normally count as income.

General Rules for Principal and Income

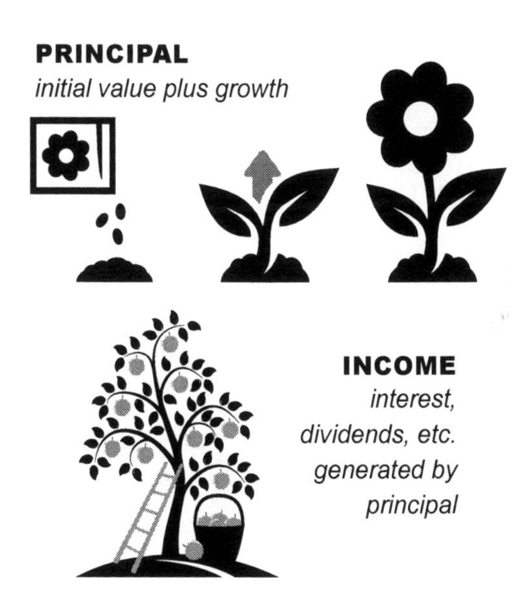

As you can imagine, this variable definition of income can have some very practical implications. First, it leaves open a potential conflict between income beneficiaries who would want income to be defined as broadly as possible, and principal recipients who would want the opposite. Second, imagine that our example trust that holds one stock has a provision that says income is to be distributed to a current beneficiary while principal is to be kept intact for the future benefit of the remainderperson. When the stock issues a dividend it will go to the current beneficiary as income. If the stock is sold, the proceeds will be added to principal and the income beneficiary receives nothing. The trust will be responsible to pay tax on the gain in principal, while the beneficiary must report and pay income on the dividend. One stock, one dividend, one sale. Two tax returns. Complicated, right? This is one area that you'll want to explore more fully in Part II, and you could definitely benefit from some professional advice to keep you on track. For now, just be comforted that you at least know that income and principal, and the difference between them, matter a lot.

Now that you have an idea of the concept, terminology, key parties, and purpose of your trust, it is time to focus more specifically on what you must do in your role as trustee.

PART II

Trustee's Responsibilities and Duties

Trustees have both *responsibilities* (day to day work) and *duties* (overarching legal guidelines).

WHAT ARE THE TRUSTEE'S RESPONSIBILITIES?

You have probably figured out by now that you have a very important part to play and there are many people counting on you to do it well—starting with the settlor, the beneficiary, the remainderperson, and the law. Let's drill down a little bit to get a better sense of what this means.

The trustee's responsibilities derive from the law and the trust agreement itself. While there are of course exceptions and modern trusts are rapidly pushing the limits of traditional rules, let's start with how most trusts work. As trustee, you have three basic responsibilities: to **administer**, **invest**, and **distribute** the trust fund.

WHAT IS TRUST ADMINISTRATION?

Your first step as trustee is to get possession of the trust assets and have ownership transferred to you, as trustee. And, thus begins administration. For investments, gaining control of the assets is a relatively easy task, entailing change of title on account forms. Other assets, such as art, can be more complicated and may involve physically moving them so that you can oversee them.

Once asset ownership is transferred, you will need to keep detailed accounts listing: the identity and value of each asset at the time it is added to the trust; any income generated by it; increases or decreases in value; distributions in cash or in kind; and payments of expenses of the trust. Corporate trustees often have software programs to create and maintain these accountings. Individual trustees can find this work overwhelming; this is where getting professional help can make all the difference. In some cases, it might make sense to outsource aspects of administration and accounting to a firm specializing in those services. For those trustees who work in family offices or law or accounting firms, it may be feasible and preferable to create a tailor-made system using standard software. It should go without saying that merely receiving bank statements and throwing them in a desk drawer (which, alas, some trustees have done in the past) is unlikely to serve the purpose. Regardless of what system is chosen, the ultimate responsibility never leaves the trustee. However, the expenses of keeping these accounts may be covered by the trust fund itself, depending on the terms of the trust.

What do you do with the trust fund?

From the start, you must be sure that title to any property in the trust is in your name as trustee so it puts others (such as an investment advisor or the tax authorities) on notice that you are holding it for the benefit of someone else. Also, you must always keep the trust fund separate from any other property you own. For example, you cannot add your own cash to the trust's account, nor can you hold stocks that legally belong to the trust in your personal investment accounts, even if it might be more convenient for you to so do. Do not miss this point: Trust assets are not your property like other things you own, and they must be kept separately from everything else. One of the essential rules of a trust is that the trust funds cannot be used to pay the trustee's obligations, and thus commingling personal and trust assets is a serious violation of a trustee's duties.

The settlor will fund (or may have funded already) the trust by transferring assets to you, as trustee of the trust. In most cases, this is done with cash and investments, but trusts can also be funded with real estate, artwork, and other types of property. The trust might be funded with a nominal amount, with the bulk of the assets added over time (often at the settlor's death), or, the funding might occur all at once. You should find out what kind of assets are already in the trust or will be added to it later.

Record the initial funding of the trust on the "Your Trust" sheet. For example, assets might include an investment account, shares of a business, or a deed to a house.

When are distributions made to beneficiaries?

Each trust agreement provides directions and guidance to the trustees on when distributions may, or must, be made to beneficiaries. Some trusts provide for mandatory distributions. For example, a trust agreement might state that all income must be distributed to a beneficiary on a quarterly basis or that a percentage of trust principal must be distributed when the beneficiary reaches a certain age. The trust agreement might instead provide the trustee with full decision-making authority or discretion to decide whether and/or when distributions can be made. One common standard is tied to the U.S. tax code and states that a trustee can make distributions for the beneficiary's "health, education, maintenance, or support." Many trusts created in the last decade or so give the trustee full discretion over distributions. For those trusts, it often helps for the trustee to seek guidance from the settlor and from legal counsel on when and how discretion is meant to be exercised. Remember, though, that if you have discretion neither the settlor nor anyone else can tell you when you must, or must not, make a distribution. The "buck" stops with you.

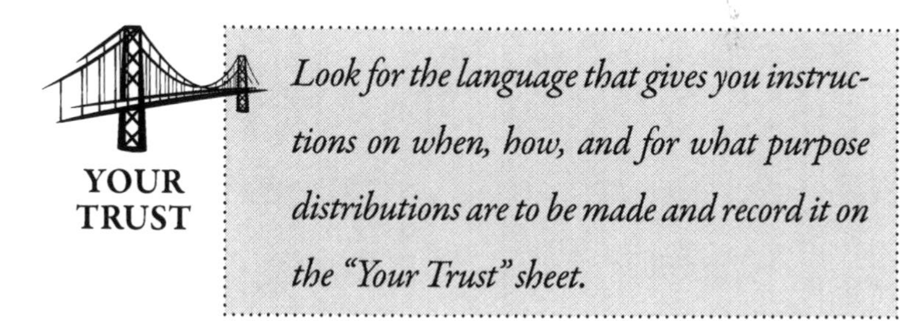

Look for the language that gives you instructions on when, how, and for what purpose distributions are to be made and record it on the "Your Trust" sheet.

In addition, and here's the rub, at all times you need to balance the interests of the beneficiaries with those of the remainderpersons. This is not easy. It requires understanding exactly how the trust was intended to be used currently and in the future. Anyone who is named in the trust with a right to receive something at the end can hold you accountable for what is left at that time. The trust might absolve you of this general rule; you must know the expectations in this regard.

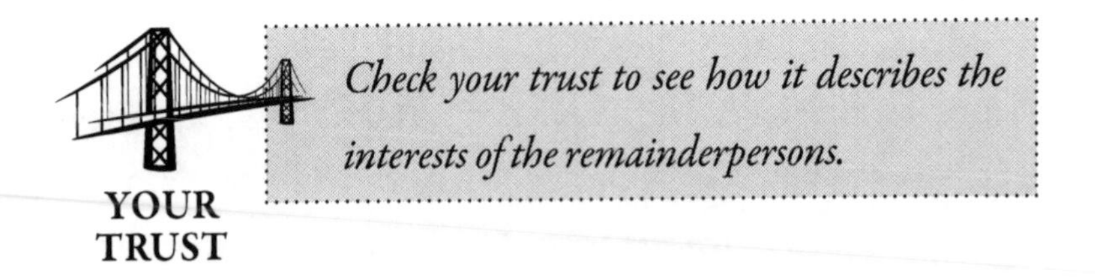

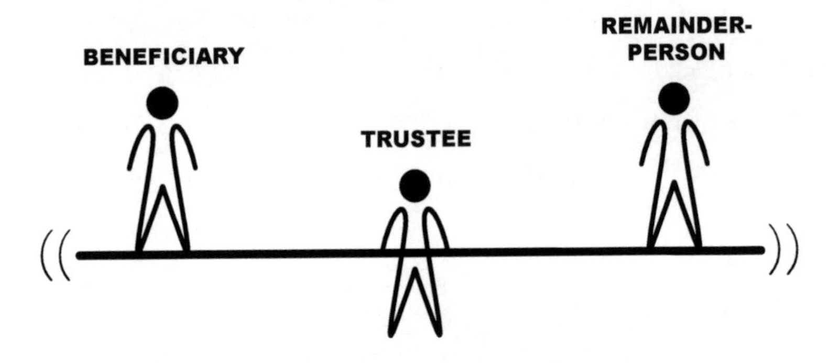

HOW SHOULD THE TRUST FUND BE INVESTED?

You may have heard that trusts must be invested very conservatively; however, times have changed and this is no longer exactly true. Traditionally, trust laws imposed a restrictive standard on how trustees could invest a trust fund. Maintenance of principal was considered paramount; growth was secondary. Specific laws varied across jurisdictions, but often this concept was enshrined in the so-called "prudent man rule," which stated that the trustee was required to invest as a prudent man would invest his own assets. Since it might have been too difficult to find (or imagine) a prudent man, some laws used a list of approved investments, which left a trustee with little or no choice over how to invest the trust fund. This system worked pretty well so long as there were investments available that could provide income, as defined for trust purposes, for current income beneficiaries and have enough growth for principal beneficiaries and remainderpersons.

Over time, however, these limitations were found to be excessively restrictive, especially for beneficiaries who needed more income and/or for remainderpersons who received the "crumbs" (in their opinion) at the end. At the same time, the investment world was evolving in ways that changed the thinking on how to invest successfully. To simplify, imagine a time when a trustee had two main investment options for a trust fund: bonds and stocks. Bonds could be counted on to produce steady income—maybe not a lot, but the returns were reliable and would satisfy most income beneficiaries. Stocks could provide some income through dividends, and the trustee could generate growth in principal as the stocks increased in value and were later sold. Things worked pretty well, until they did not.

In the latter half of the twentieth century, successful companies (think Microsoft) started issuing stocks that grew rapidly with skyrocketing prices, but they did not issue any dividends. At the same time, bonds became less of a sure bet for steady income, especially when measured after inflation, which reduced the buying power of bond returns. Trustees trying to get income and growth were in a bind. If they invested in stocks that didn't issue dividends, under trust accounting rules they did not have income that they could distribute to income beneficiaries. Yet they could please the principal beneficiaries and remainderpersons, who received more principal when the stock prices rose. A trustee who decided to stay away from growth stocks had fewer attractive investments so trust returns fell behind. If this wasn't hard enough, the investment world became more complex with the proliferation of investment vehicles, including hedge funds and alternative assets such as real estate. Further, a new investment theory known as *modern portfolio theory* declared that investment results depended more on how assets were allocated overall within a portfolio than on the returns of any particular investment. Stock picking was not the way to invest successfully over time; asset allocation became the new lens through which trustees were expected to invest and would be judged.

Modern Portfolio Theory

Trustees rightfully became worried about their liability as they invested in this rapidly changing world. As in the Middle Ages, people went to the courts to sort things out, which alerted legislatures to the need to resolve these new problems. Toward the end of the twentieth century, a general trend in the law fundamentally changed the way that trustees can and should invest. This trend is now embodied in the Prudent Investor Rule and the Principal and Income Act.

The Prudent Investor Rule adopted a more flexible and comprehensive framework than the prudent man rule. The trustee is now tested on the overall strategy, looking across the entire portfolio at risk and *total return* (performance as measured by both asset value growth and any income generated). Diversification among asset classes has become the guiding principle, with the total return of the trust being paramount. This may sound like common sense, but at the time it was somewhat revolutionary in the field.

Prudent Investor Rule

What does this mean for your approach to investments as a trustee? No more approved list, no more looking at whether a particular stock that doesn't pay dividends would be suitable for a trust with a beneficiary entitled to income distributions. Under the total return concept, the results for the entire portfolio—growth and income—are what matter. The Prudent Investor Rule also made clear that trustees are permitted to delegate their investment responsibility to a third party, so long as the delegation is done in a prudent manner and the actions of the third party are regularly reviewed by the trustee.

This sounded like a great solution for trustees. The distinction between income and principal should become much less important because, after all, stocks can be sold to generate cash as needed. But, once again, complications arose for trusts that required distributions of some sort of income. While a trustee was entitled to invest on a total return basis, traditional fiduciary accounting still distinguished between income and principal, and the cash proceeds from selling stock did not meet the definition of income. So, the trustee could invest in Microsoft but couldn't pay the income beneficiary from a successful increase in value because the stock didn't pay dividends. A trustee was still restricted to treating only interest and dividends as income.

In response to these challenges, all of the popular jurisdictions for managing trusts adopted new rules under the Principal and Income Act that were intended to ensure that investments chosen for total return (including stocks that did not issue dividends) would not adversely affect income beneficiaries. The new rules gave trustees the ability to make adjustments between what is considered income and what is considered principal for trust accounting purposes. In some cases, trustees are allowed to choose a specific percentage (the *unitrust amount*) of the trust fund to be considered income for distribution purposes.

As a result of these developments, generally speaking, trustees now have far more flexibility in the investments they choose and the ways they account for the portions of the trust fund that are considered income and principal for distribution and accounting purposes. Sounds great, right? Well, you won't be surprised to learn that it is more complicated still. These laws don't apply everywhere in the same way, and some trusts have assets that don't fit well into this system. For example, trusts that are intended to own a single asset such as a family business often exempt the trustee from the rules and specifically allow trustees to hold a single asset, namely the business. Some trusts take advantage of still further legal changes, including the ability to set a unitrust amount as trust income. Other trusts make no distinction between income and principal but are funded with assets that are difficult to value and sell. As trustee, you will need to know which law applies to the investments in your trust.

This would be a good time to record whether there are any special provisions either subjecting you to or relieving you from the Prudent Investor Rule or requiring that you hold onto assets such as a family business.

WHAT ARE THE TRUSTEE'S DUTIES?*

As trustee, you are considered a *fiduciary* who is subject to a set of duties with respect to how you handle your role. These duties are defined by broad guidelines on how you must act in carrying out your responsibilities. It is easy to get lost in day-to-day tasks, but be careful lest you forget the overriding duties by which you will be judged. Here are some of the most important duties that you should always have in mind when you are serving as trustee, with the caveat that of course there are exceptions. The examples below are merely illustrative of how they might apply. You should seek legal advice anytime you think you might be engaging in a transaction that might put one at risk.

1. Duty of Loyalty. The trustee must administer the trust solely in the interest of the beneficiaries and must avoid conflicts of interest. Speaking generally, this means that a trustee may

* This section draws heavily, and gratefully, from Richards and Gross, *The Trustee's Guide* (cited in Resources), which provides more detail and guidance for trustees.

not enter into a transaction with the trust in which the trustee receives a financial benefit. In some cases, this means that even the appearance of or opportunity for personal gain must be avoided. So, if the trustee owns a business, it would be considered a violation of the duty of loyalty to have the trust buy shares of the business because the trustee would benefit financially from the transaction. A trustee may not use trust assets for the trustee's own benefit. Simply put, you can't pay your personal bills with the trust fund, even if you intend to pay the trust back very soon.

2. Duty to Deal Impartially with Beneficiaries. Unless the trust agreement provides otherwise, the trustee cannot favor one beneficiary over another. For example, if your trust has a group of beneficiaries who are entitled to receive equal distributions from trust income, you must divide the income among them, even if you like one beneficiary more than the others or think that person's use for the money is more "worthy." In addition, as trustee you have to be careful not to favor current beneficiaries over the interests of remainderpersons who will come later (unless of course the trust agreement tells you to do so).

3. Duty to Take and Control Trust Property. As discussed above, the trustee must take possession and legal control of the trust fund. You may arrange for safekeeping and custody of the trust fund to be held by third parties; for example, you could use a bank as custodian of the trust investment account.

4. Duty to Keep Trust Property Segregated. The trustee must hold each trust account separately and cannot commingle assets of different trusts or mix the trust fund together with the trustee's personal assets.

5. Duty to Preserve Trust Property. The trustee must obtain proper insurance for tangible personal and real property and must maintain proper supervision of trust assets in investment accounts.

6. Duty to Make the Trust Property Productive. A trustee cannot hold onto property that is not producing income for beneficiaries or does not have a likelihood of capital appreciation. Note, however, that despite this general duty, the trust agreement may direct the trustee to hold onto an asset (for example, shares of a family business) and may relieve the trustee of liability for holding such property.

7. Duty to Pay Income to Beneficiaries. The trustee must follow the instructions of the trust, but should not wait for unreasonable periods of time to pay income that is due to beneficiaries.

8. Duty to Keep and Render Accounts. While the trust agreement or governing law usually address the requirements for formal or informal accountings or other means of providing information to beneficiaries, the general rule is that the trustee is responsible for maintaining information on the trust funds and accounts in a form that can be made available to the beneficiaries upon request or periodically. Depending on applicable laws and the trust agreement, beneficiaries may be able to go to court to compel a formal accounting and the trustee must prove that his or her actions with the trust fund have been in accord with the trust agreement.

9. Duty to Furnish Information. As indicated above, the beneficiary has the right to make reasonable demands of the trustee to receive information that is relevant to the beneficiary's interest in the trust. Note, however, that some states and other jurisdictions have enacted laws that allow the trust agreement to restrict the beneficiary's right to trust information.

You will want to know your legal obligations or restrictions on providing information to beneficiaries.

10. Duty to Exercise Reasonable Care and Skill. The trustee must exercise the level of prudence and care that an ordinary person would; however, in some states the trustee is held to a higher standard. Also, the trust agreement will often establish the applicable standard for liability for the trustee. There is a general trend toward greater protection of trustees, but each trust will be judged by its own terms and applicable law.

You should review your trust agreement and find out the standard that applies to you.

11. Duty Not to Delegate. Generally speaking, a trustee cannot delegate his or her responsibilities; the trustee is ultimately liable for all actions with respect to trust administration. While this prohibition on delegation of duty has been a longstanding tenet of trust law, in recent decades a number of states have passed laws allowing delegation of some essential trustee duties. Some states even allow responsibility for investment, administration, and distribution to be divided among different parties, including some who are not named trustees but are held to the same standards. The devil is in the details, and it is best to know the boundaries of your responsibilities, especially if you have a co-trustee, as soon as possible.

12. Duty to Enforce Claims. If the trust has a claim against a third party, the trustee has a duty to the trust beneficiaries to pursue the claim. For example, if the trust enters into a transaction with a contractor who fails to perform on a contract, the trustee must determine whether and how to pursue a claim against the contractor.

13. Duty to Defend Actions. If the trust is the subject of a claim, the trustee owes an obligation to trust beneficiaries to defend the trust with respect to the claim and to protect the trust fund. Most trust agreements specifically provide that the costs of such defense are to be paid out of the trust fund.

14. Duty Concerning Co-Trustees. Even if there are several co-trustees, each trustee has responsibility to the trust beneficiaries. Delegation and division of duties between co-trustees must be done carefully to prevent the trustee from violating this fiduciary duty.

If you have a co-trustee, it is important to understand the division of your responsibilities and how any disagreements are to be resolved.

15. Duty with Respect to Individuals Having Control Powers. So long as there is no conflict with the trustee's own duty to the trust, the trustee must take instructions from those with legal authority and power to issue it. For example, your trust might provide that the grantor can revoke the trust without your consent. If so, you must comply.

Take a look through your trust agreement. You might find a long list of powers and duties. Remember these provisions, and refer to them when you have questions about what you can, and can't, do in a particular situation.

PART III

*The Beneficiary**

As trustee, you alone cannot make the trust a success. Much depends on the beneficiary, and how you work together. You are probably familiar with the term "trust fund baby," used to describe individuals who live on, or at least have their lifestyles excessively supplemented by, distributions from family trusts. Sadly, some of these people seem to live in perpetual childhood or adolescence,

* This section draws from prior writings by the author, and James E. Hughes, Jr., individually and together. See citations in Resources.

and this is in no small part due to the way their trusts are handled. You probably do not want to create this kind of situation with your trust. However, it is a very real possibility, and how you function as trustee can have a profound impact on whether or not this happens.

You must remember that you do not take the place of a beneficiary's parent just because you are serving as trustee. This is easier to remember when the beneficiary is already an adult but can be a challenge at any age, given the dynamic between the two positions. The trustee's role is somewhere along the lines of parent, sibling, aunt, or uncle, but is really none of these. It is more, and less, than family, requiring a certain unconditional support backed up by the legal framework of the trust.

You will have to work hard to make the trust a positive experience in the beneficiary's life, and herein lies the heart of the matter. You must do your work *in relationship with* the beneficiary. Neither of you will ever be totally in the right or in the wrong. How you set the tone and balance things with the beneficiary will make all the difference. It is essential that you think about the beneficiary's position with compassion. Beneficiaries can sense when you fail to understand their personal difficulties as much as when you show support and encouragement.

What is the beneficiary's position?

A beneficiary is in a complicated position; it will help both of you to explore it deeply. Some beneficiaries might have emotional and psychological limitations, and many are still minor children. Even the most competent must come to terms with the reality of beneficial ownership, which is a strange concept that feels limiting to most people. A trust is legally shared ownership that can create positive opportunities, but it also can be viewed as a barrier to freedom and independence. Legal ownership gives the trustee acknowledged authority with the outside world; beneficial ownership is often more an internal state of mind that can feel unrecognized by third parties. It can make even the most mature beneficiary feel infantilized. If you do not want that to happen, you'll need to encourage the beneficiary to understand how you can both work toward a mature relationship with each other and with the trust.

A trustee who creates an open, transparent environment is more likely to succeed in the ultimate goal of truly helping the beneficiary. This means keeping lines of communication open at all times and asking questions as much as or even more than giving answers. A trustee who encourages the beneficiary to take an active part in the trust is more likely to have a true partner in the process. The trustee can lead this way by making sure that the beneficiary has access to trust information and understands not just the financial but also the emotional implications of being a beneficiary. Sometimes the trustee will need to refer the beneficiary to educational resources on issues ranging from financial matters to psychological challenges. A trustee who is already comfortable with these issues will be far more equipped to assist the beneficiary as well. Technical prowess is important, but it takes more than that. Empathy matters. It also helps if you always keep in mind that a beneficiary has rights and responsibilities, just as you do.

What are the beneficiary's rights?

A beneficiary's rights derive both from trust law and the specific terms of a trust agreement. Somewhat surprisingly, the range of these rights can be quite varied. In some jurisdictions and many trusts, the rights of beneficiaries are extremely restricted. In those cases, beneficiaries are hardly allowed to know that a trust exists for their benefit, much less do they have any way to force a trustee to be accountable to them. In others, the settlor may provide far more authority to beneficiaries, often limited only as needed to prevent potentially adverse tax consequences.

For most trusts, beneficiaries have considerable rights that have been in the law for centuries. This is key to the concept of a trust—that is, recognizing and respecting that people who do not have legal ownership can nonetheless benefit from these special legal arrangements. Given the essentially private nature of the relationship, it often falls to the trustee to ensure that the beneficiary's rights are respected. This may require the trustee not only to acknowledge when a beneficiary exerts valid rights, but also to proactively outline rights of which the beneficiary might not be aware. Indeed, in the past decade or so there has been a growing movement among professionals and families to raise awareness of the rights of beneficiaries. This is part of a broader effort to reduce the likelihood of creating those so-called trust fund babies and to make sure that trusts enhance beneficiaries' lives rather than drag them down. If you wish to serve well as trustee, it will help for you to keep these rights in mind at all times and proactively seek to make them real.

Most importantly, beneficiaries should feel that they have the right to be heard. This starts with being able to ask questions and describe life experiences in a way that is neither judged nor dismissed. It is highly unlikely that a beneficiary will have the same worldview or make the same life choices as a trustee. This should be a point of interest and exploration for the trustee and an opportunity to learn about the beneficiary's true life experience. To be an active participant, a beneficiary should have the opportunity to review the trust agreement and related documents, so long as this is not prohibited by law or the agreement itself. A beneficiary has a right to expect the trustee to be willing to maintain open communication during the entire term of the trust. This is not easy work, and many of the questions might be hard to answer.

Each beneficiary should know that the trustee is accountable to the beneficiary, and also to all other beneficiaries and remainderpersons. This will play out in how you, as trustee, respond to beneficiary requests for information and how you explain why you take specific actions. Beneficiaries should have a right to meet with their trustees annually and have at least quarterly check-ins as well.

As the expression goes, "What's good for the goose is good for the gander." A trustee will likely be thinking about the beneficiary's performance, rightfully or not. At the same time, the beneficiary has a right to openly discuss the trustee's performance and make suggestions about what would work better. This should not be seen as an opportunity to blindly criticize but rather a chance to explain behavior and make changes where it makes sense. Neither party should feel beholden to the other. Personal styles will differ, and making an effort to meet in the middle will help beneficiary and trustee alike.

By following these best practices, there should be no need for a trustee to feel under attack or for a beneficiary to feel marginalized. However, it is certainly possible that conflict will arise in the relationship. If that's the case, there are several steps to take. First, honestly assessing whether the complaints are warranted is a good starting point for both sides. Searching together for a compromise in which the trustee can still meet responsibilities and duties in accommodation with the beneficiary's concerns should be the next step for trustee and beneficiary. At all times it is important to recognize that beneficiaries may be just as—if not more—at fault than the trustee. Finally, however, if a trustee has failed to perform professionally, a beneficiary should be able to seek removal of the trustee. This "last resort" should be just that, and beneficiaries who have good relationships with trustees rarely ask for it. For tax and other reasons, beneficiaries can rarely demand removal, but the ability to voice concern is legitimate and important.

You must be aware of and support your beneficiaries' rights, as well as their responsibilities. If you start off by letting a beneficiary off the hook, you will both likely pay the price later. Similarly, if you defer to the beneficiary too much you will not be meeting your duties.

What are the beneficiary's responsibilities?

Beneficiaries should not feel that a trust is a free ride and that distributions will arrive in the mail without any effort on their part. As trustee, you will need to help beneficiaries understand that they too, have responsibilities and it is in their best interests to fulfill them. First and foremost, beneficiaries must be active participants in the trust experience. This starts with understanding the trust purpose and reviewing to the extent possible the salient terms of the trust agreement. Beneficiaries should also generally understand the holdings in the trust fund, whether they are investments, art, real estate, a family business, or some other form of property.

There is no ideal background for a beneficiary, and often those with nontraditional training can grasp the trust concept better than their peers who might appear more suited to the task. Emotional maturity and a willingness to learn are more important than technical legal or financial knowledge. It is important to build on a beneficiary's strengths and natural talents. Creatively find a way to work together. Help your beneficiaries understand how their rights and responsibilities relate to those held by you, other beneficiaries, and the remainderpersons.

There is a certain level of comprehension that will be useful for any beneficiary to master. This includes gaining a basic understanding of trust law, as well as investment fundamentals. Beneficiaries do not need to be experts, but can certainly learn about modern portfolio theory, the Prudent Investor Rule, and some of the ways in which the trustee must balance demands for income and growth in a portfolio. Some appreciation of the complexities of trust accounting will help, as well as awareness of the tax issues related to the trust. Finally, exposure to how and why the trustee and other professionals are compensated could help a beneficiary gain an appreciation of the complicated professional aspects of the tasks at hand.

These are merely general guidelines, which can and should lead to conversations with the beneficiary. It is also an area where you can and should seek help from outside resources—and not just legal advice. It's hard to understate the depth of emotional complexity in a trustee-beneficiary relationship. Take this as an opportunity to learn and grow; the positive effects will flow to the beneficiaries as well.

How can trustees support beneficiaries?

There are many ways that you can support beneficiaries so that they can make the most of their position. At a minimum, make sure that you meet personally with each beneficiary at least once a year, and by phone every quarter. In those meetings, get to know how the beneficiary is doing in life and don't just focus on the financials. No one can be reduced to simple needs and distribution requests, and the more you find a way to set a tone of partnership with the beneficiary the more likely you will both enjoy your experience. Follow an agenda that balances some formality with the reality that the issues you are discussing are highly personal. Make sure the beneficiary is an active participant in your work together.

PART IV

Final Questions

Before you agree to accept your appointment or to continue acting as trustee, take a moment to consider these very important questions.

When will the trust end?

A trust has a defined beginning, middle, and end. An inter vivos trust generally begins when it is signed. A testamentary trust (under a will) generally starts upon the death of the person who wrote the will (known as the *testator*.) Most trusts end upon the occurrence of a particular event; for example, the death of a beneficiary. Historically, almost all trusts (excluding charitable ones) had to end at some point, but now many trusts can last forever—these are often called dynasty or perpetual trusts. Today, most trusts are still limited by law to a maximum *perpetuities period*, which usually states that the trust may not last more than one lifetime (starting at the time the trust is created) plus an additional 21 years. Essentially, this means that if a trust does not by its terms end sooner, it must end approximately 80–100 years after it begins.

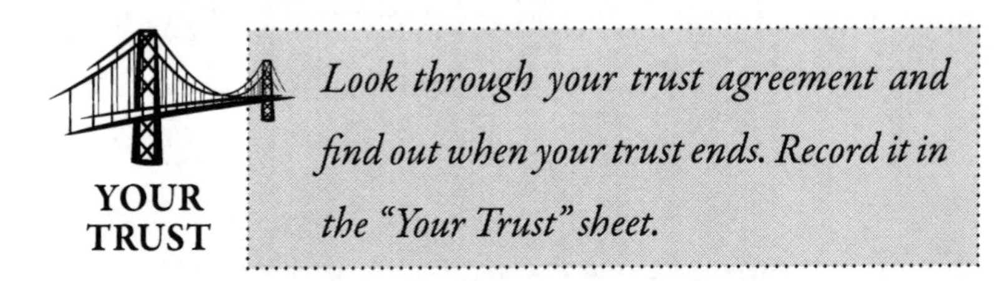

Look through your trust agreement and find out when your trust ends. Record it in the "Your Trust" sheet.

Can I be paid?

Given how much responsibility and work fall upon a trustee, it seems only fair that the position be compensated. Indeed, the law often provides guidelines for compensation, and most trust agreements either refer to the law or include specific provisions on it. At the same time, some trusts are silent on the issue, while others specifically prohibit compensation for family members who serve as trustee. In all these cases, however, the trust fund should be available to pay for legitimate expenses of the trust, such as taxes, court filing fees, and expenses of legal counsel.

Look through your trust agreement to see whether, and how, trustee fees and trust expenses are covered. Record this in the "Your Trust" sheet.

What's the worst that could happen?

By now, you should be feeling a little better, or at least more informed about what it means to be a trustee. But you might still have a gnawing feeling that it isn't for you, and you may not have forgotten those scary stories you have heard. Before going further, it's worth considering the potential risks in more detail. Liability can come in many forms.

The first and most difficult risk is to the very relationship that got you into this position in the first place. No matter what your relationship was like in the past, it will never be the same. You will go from being a family member, friend, confidante, or professional advisor to someone with very serious legal rights and responsibilities. Not only will you have authority that is based in the law, there are also emotional and practical issues that can be quite difficult to navigate. You might have to say no to friends or relatives when you know that a distribution wouldn't be in their best interests.

You might also start to feel resentful when you have to be the "grown up" all the time. It might start to feel like the beneficiary gets to have all the fun while you carry all the burdens.

There is also a risk that you will start to feel that you have a great deal of power and, consciously or not, start to exercise it in ways that create problems for the beneficiary or others involved. Over time, you might lose compassion for a beneficiary whose lifestyle and behavior differ from your own. You might even wonder whether you are contributing to that behavior or making the beneficiary dependent on your generosity. This is not an easy position to be in, and you would do well to get some help with the psychological and emotional challenges of your role.

Second, the trust will take time, and a lot of it. If you are appointed trustee in the context of an existing professional relationship, you will need to figure out how to integrate your responsibilities into your work life so that you are not putting your day job at risk. If you serve as trustee for a family member or friend, you'll have to find a way to carve out time against conflicting priorities on nights and weekends. It might feel like you have to decide between time for your own family and personal life vs. the needs of the trust and its beneficiaries.

Third, you will be held to a very high standard under the law, and if you are found to have failed to meet it, despite your best intentions, you can be sued. That can cost you both money—potentially a lot—and time.

Finally, you might ask yourself whether you are ready to take on this level of responsibility at this point in your life. Do you feel too young or old? What about the potential liability for your family? Take time to do some honest soul searching. There is no shame in saying no or resigning, but there is great risk in doing the job halfheartedly.

What comes next?

If you've made it this far, you are at a critical juncture. If you are comfortable with what you've heard, then it is time to get on with the real work and get the additional help you need to do it. If reading this has made you even more uncertain, it is probably time to get help assessing your alternatives. There are a number of ways to minimize potential liability by ensuring that you meet all duties as well as possible, handle administration professionally, foster healthy relationships with beneficiaries, have regular meetings with counsel, and document decisions, among other things. You can also try to obtain insurance to cover your liability, although the options tend to be limited. The trust agreement itself may also provide you additional protections.

However, by law and as a practical matter, there is no way to eliminate all potential liability or to obtain indemnification or insurance to cover it completely. If after a review of your options, you decide that the risks are too much for you to bear—personally, professionally, or financially—you should find out how you can decline the appointment or resign if you are already acting as trustee. The trust agreement will likely outline a process; if not, the law will. In either case, it would be best to seek legal counsel on what you can do in your situation.

If you choose to continue as trustee, then you will join many who have gone before you. While they might have found it challenging, they can attest to the fact that there is little else in life that involves similar intellectual, emotional, and professional accomplishments and rewards. The potential to have a meaningful impact on the lives of your beneficiaries and yourself is immeasurable.

Good luck!

Resources

Angus, Patricia M., *Ten Facts Every Trust Beneficiary Should Know*, Private Wealth Management, Campden Publishing, 2005.

Ascher, Scott, Wakeman, *Ascher and Scott on Trusts*, Fifth Edition, Aspen Publishers, New York, New York, 2010.

Bove, Alexander A. Jr., Esq., *The Complete Book of Wills, Estates and Trusts*, Henry Holt and Company, LLC, New York, New York, 2005.

Goldstone, Hartley, James E. Hughes, Jr. and Keith Whitaker, *Family Trusts*, John Wiley & Sons, Hoboken, New Jersey, 2016.

Goldstone, Hartley and Kathy Wiseman, *Trustworthy*, Trustscape LLC, Denver, Colorado, 2012.

Hughes, James E., Jr., *Family Wealth: Keeping It in the Family*, Bloomberg Press, Princeton, New Jersey, 2004.

Rounds, Charles E. Jr. and Charles E. Rounds, III, *Loring and Rounds: A Trustee's Handbook*, CCH Incorporated, New York, New York, 2015.

Restatement of the Law Third, Trusts 3rd, American Law Institute, Philadelphia, Pennsylvania, 1992.

Shenkman, Martin M., *The Complete Book of Trusts*, John Wiley & Sons, Inc., New York, New York, 2002.

Train, John and Melfe, Thomas A., *Investing and Managing Trusts under the New Prudent Investor Rule*, Harvard Business School Press, Boston, Massachusetts, 1999.

Richards, Pierre E. and Gross, Howard I., Esq., *The Trustee's Guide: A Handbook for Individual Trustees, Beneficiaries, and Advisors*, Tower Publishing, Standish, Maine, 1999.

YOUR TRUST	
Name of Trust	
Purpose(s) of Trust	
Date of Trust	
Settlor	
Trustee(s)	
Current	
Successor(s)	
Ways of changing trustee	
Beneficiaries	
Income	
Principal	
Terms of Trust	
Distribution provisions	
Other important provisions	
Special restrictions	
Termination	

YOUR TRUST	
Trust Investments	
Party responsible for investing	
Investment guidelines	
Who receives investment statements	
Jurisdiction	
Governing Law	
Compensation	

Questions/Notes

About the Author

PATRICIA M. ANGUS, ESQ., is committed to helping create a better future. For more than two decades, she has been a thought leader in family enterprise, wealth, governance, and philanthropy. She practiced trusts and estates law and served as a wealth advisor to families globally before establishing Angus Advisory Group LLC. She is an adjunct professor at Columbia University Business School, authors the Building Bridges column on www.wealthmanagement.com, and is a member of the *Trusts & Estates* Family Businesses Committee.

Visit her website at:
www.angusadvisorygroup.com.

Made in the USA
Middletown, DE
13 October 2016